Renewable & Nonrenewable Resources

A Compare and Contrast Book

Natural Resources come from the Earth. Plants, animals, air, sunlight, water, soil, oil, natural gas, coal, rocks, and minerals are natural resources. These resources are used to make everything we use.

Renewable resources are easily made and replaced within a period of time usually shorter than a person's lifetime.

Nonrenewable resources cannot be easily replaced as it takes much longer than a human lifetime to make new.

Living things provide us with renewable resources. Plants and animals make more of themselves with or without human help.

Farmers plant fields of fruit, vegetables, and grains that we eat. They save seeds to plant more.

Some people even grow some of their own food in a garden.

Animals give birth to young and then the young grow into adults to make more baby animals. Whether raised on farms or found in the wild, animals provide us with renewable resources.

It takes the Earth up to hundreds of thousands, if not millions, of years to make some of the nonrenewable resources we use. When those resources are gone, or we can't find anymore, we must do without or use substitutes that we can make (synthetics) from other resources.

We use three main nonrenewable fossil fuels for energy: coal, oil, and natural gas. We drill and quarry to find and use these resources.

Coal is a sedimentary rock formed over millions of years from decaying plant material. Almost half of the electricity we use in the United States comes from nonrenewable coal that has been crushed and burned. As the coal burns, it creates steam that allows generators to make the electricity.

If coal is heated in a special manner, it results in a high-carbon fuel called "coke." It is not anything like the cola drink; this coke is used to make steel and iron ore.

Coal mining is tough, dirty work that can be very dangerous to the miners.

In some areas, we drill into the Earth and use high pressure to push water, sand, and chemicals into the Earth. This process, known as fracking, makes new pathways for the oil and gas to be pulled out more efficiently. That makes it less expensive for us to heat our homes or for the energy we use.

Some people are concerned that the chemicals used in fracking may get into the groundwater and may be dangerous for humans to drink. Others are concerned that fracking causes earthquakes.

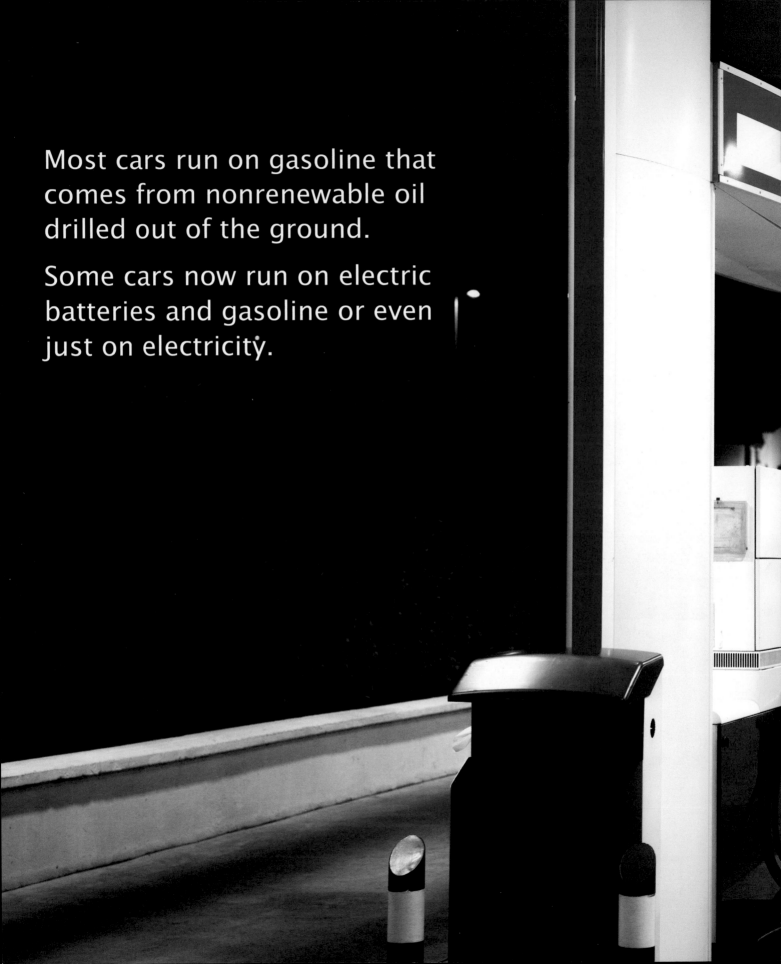

Most cars run on gasoline that comes from nonrenewable oil drilled out of the ground.

Some cars now run on electric batteries and gasoline or even just on electricity.

Where does electricity come from?

In addition to nonrenewable coal, we use renewable resources too: sunlight (solar), water, heat from the earth (geothermal), and wind.

Even if something is nonrenewable, we can reuse or recycle it.

Chances are that if you look around right now, you'll see something made of plastic. Plastic is made from oil drilled out of the ground.

Or you might have just taken a drink from an aluminum can. Aluminum is a mineral.

Because oil, rocks, and minerals are nonrenewable, we recycle plastic and aluminum to make new products.

If an old stone farmhouse is torn down, the stones can be used in other, newer buildings.

Water is a natural resource and is found under the ground (groundwater), on the surface of the earth, frozen in snow and glaciers at the poles or high in the mountains, and in the sky (clouds). Water is renewable because it is naturally recycled through the water cycle.

We should not take it for granted, though. We need fresh water to drink and survive.

Most of the water on the earth's surface is salt water. We use reverse osmosis and desalinization to change salt water into drinking water.

If water found deep in the earth is removed faster than it can be replaced, we may run out in that area.

Freshwater locations may become polluted, making it unsafe for us to use.

If we use renewable resources faster than they can renew, they can become nonrenewable. For example, if we catch so many fish in any given area, there may not be enough fish left to repopulate that area.

But if we make sure to leave enough fish in an area to be able to repopulate, then the fish are sustainable and renewable.

If we pollute or destroy the habitat, the fish may not survive, becoming nonrenewable in that area.

If we cut down all the trees in an area to build houses, but it takes 40 to 50 years for new trees to be big enough to use for lumber, then we run out of trees to use in that area. Lumber will have to be trucked in from other areas or other resources used instead.

Many logging companies are now careful to plant trees, or to not clear cut areas to keep the forests sustainable.

Even when resources are renewable, we still need to conserve and care for them.

For Creative Minds

Renewable or Not?

Can you identify which of these things come from renewable or nonrenewable resources?

Discuss with a friend or an adult what resources were used and how we get them.

corn chips

plastic

peanut butter

gasoline

grape jelly

turkey

Answers: Renewable: corn chips, peanut butter, grape jelly, turkey
Nonrenewable: plastic (recyclable), gasoline

stone steps

vegetables

diamond ring

wood blocks

stone tiles

chicken nuggets

aluminum cans

rubber tire

wood lumber

Answers: Renewable: vegetables, wood blocks, chicken nuggets, rubber tire, wood lumber
Nonrenewable: stone steps, diamond ring, stone tiles, aluminum cans (recyclable)

Resource Conservation: Reduce, Reuse, or Recycle

It's important to conserve resources, especially nonrenewable resources.

Sometimes the easiest way to conserve a resource is by reducing the need for it.

Sometimes, it's very easy to reuse something for either the same purpose or something new and different.

Cardboard, aluminum, plastic, and glass are all things that are easily recycled.

Discuss your answers to the following questions with a friend or family member.

Describe what it means to reduce the need for something.	Describe what it means to reuse something.	Describe what it means to recycle something.	What are some ways you can reduce water usage on daily?	Describe how you can recycle a favorite toy when you outgrow it.
In what can you carry a lunch each day instead of a plastic or paper bag?	What are some ways you can reuse or recycle clothes you have outgrown?	What are some ways you can reduce use of plastic water bottles?	What are some ways you can conserve (reduce) electricity in your house?	What are some ways you can reduce the need for wrapping paper?
How can you reduce using plastic bags from the grocery store?	Describe things you can make with paper towel or toilet paper holders.	What are some things that can be recycled?	Does your town or city provide recycling?	How would you recycle things?

Electricity

As mentioned in the book, which of the following resources might be used to make electricity?

wind

water

sun (solar)

coal

Answers: All

Thanks to Chip Lindsey, Senior Director of Education at the Children's Museum of Pittsburgh, for verifying the accuracy of the information in this book.

Unless otherwise noted, all photographs are licensed through Adobe Stock Photos or Shutterstock.

Library of Congress Cataloging-in-Publication Data

Title: Renewable or nonrenewable resources : a compare and contrast book.
Description: Mt. Pleasant, SC : Arbordale Publishing, LLC, 2021. | Series: Compare and contrast book | Includes bibliographical references.
Identifiers: LCCN 2021013711 (print) | LCCN 2021013712 (ebook) | ISBN 9781643519807 (paperback) | ISBN 9781638170181 (adobe pdf) | ISBN 9781638170372 (epub) | ISBN 9781643519999 (interactive, dual-language, read-aloud ebook)
Subjects: LCSH: Recycling (Waste, etc.)--Juvenile literature. | Renewable natural resources--Juvenile literature.
Classification: LCC TD794.5 .R4445 2021 (print) | LCC TD794.5 (ebook) | DDC 333.7--dc23
LC record available at https://lccn.loc.gov/2021013711
LC ebook record available at https://lccn.loc.gov/2021013712

Lexile® Level: 990L

Bibliography

Dews, Fred. "The Economic Benefits of Fracking." Brookings, Brookings, 23 Mar. 2015, www.brookings.edu/blog/brookings-now/2015/03/23/the-economic-benefits-of-fracking/.

"Fracking, Oil and Gas Development." American Rivers, www.americanrivers.org/threats-solutions/energy-development/fracking/.

King, Hobart M. "Coal: Anthracite, Bituminous, Coke, Pictures, Formation, Uses." Geology.com, 2019, geology.com/rocks/coal.shtml.

Kopp, Otto C. "Coal | Facts, Uses, & Types." Encyclopædia Britannica, 18 Jan. 2019, www.britannica.com/science/coal-fossil-fuel.

National Geographic Society. "Renewable Resources." National Geographic Society, 31 May 2019, www.nationalgeographic.org/encyclopedia/renewable-resources/.

"Reuse." Kids Environment Kids Health - National Institute of Environmental Health Sciences, kids.niehs.nih.gov/topics/reduce/reuse/index.htm.

Stark, Kevin. "Renewable and Non-Renewable Energy Resources Explained." KQED, 6 Sept. 2019, www.kqed.org/science/renewable-and-non-renewable-energy-resources-explained.

Types of Coal Mining. 2011, feeco.com/types-coal-mining/.

U.S. Energy Information Administration. "Renewable Energy Explained - U.S. Energy Information Administration (EIA)." Eia.gov, 2016, www.eia.gov/energyexplained/renewable-sources/.

"What Is Coal Used For?" Usgs.gov, 2012, www.usgs.gov/faqs/what-coal-used?qt-news_science_products=0#qt-news_science_products.

Printed in the US
This product conforms to CPSIA 2008
First Printing

Arbordale Publishing, LLC
Mt. Pleasant, SC 29464
www.ArbordalePublishing.com